Pieces to Play

with

Step by Step

by

Edna Mae Burnam

To my dear friend, Pauline Cruickshank

CONTENTS

Book
ISBN 978-1-4234-3599-0

Book/CD
ISBN 978-1-4234-3616-4

WILLIS MUSIC

EXCLUSIVELY DISTRIBUTED BY

HAL•LEONARD®
CORPORATION
7777 W. BLUEMOUND RD. P.O. BOX 13819 MILWAUKEE, WI 53213

T005G144

Visit Hal Leonard Online at
www.halleonard.com

TO THE TEACHER

The pieces in this book have been composed to correlate exactly with the Edna Mae Burnam Piano Course STEP BY STEP—Book Six. Prefixed to each piece is an indication of the exact page of STEP BY STEP—Book Six at which a selection from PIECES TO PLAY may be introduced. When the student reaches this page, he/she is ready to play with ease and understanding.

All of the pieces in this book may serve as repertoire for the student at this level.

The pieces in this book should be:

1. Perfected;
2. Memorized;
3. Played with expression and poise;
4. Kept in readiness to play for company.

Edna Mae Burnam

The student is ready to play this piece when he has reached page 10 of
Edna Mae Burnam's STEP BY STEP - Book Six.

THE HORSE SHOW

By EDNA MAE BURNAM

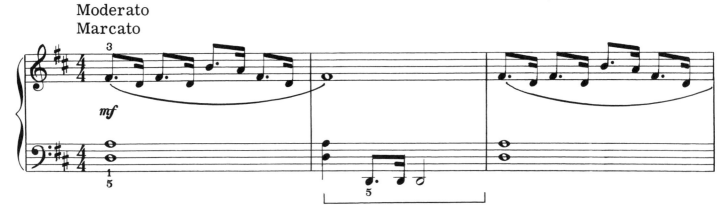

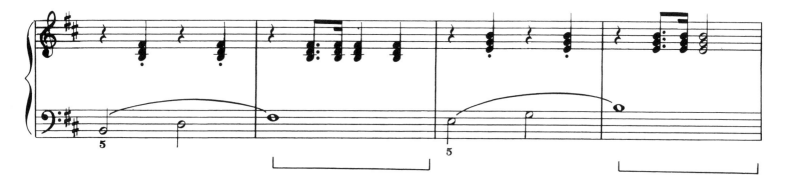

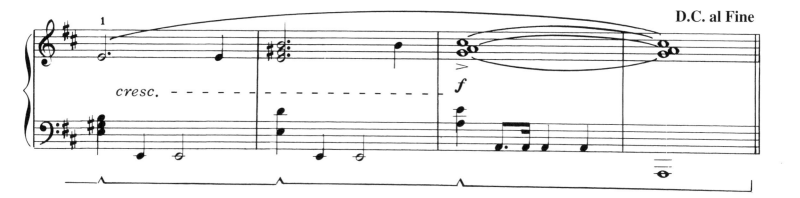

The student is ready to play this piece when he has reached page 16 of
Edna Mae Burnam's STEP BY STEP – Book Six.

THE STARS ARE COMING OUT

By EDNA MAE BURNAM

Moderato
Dolce

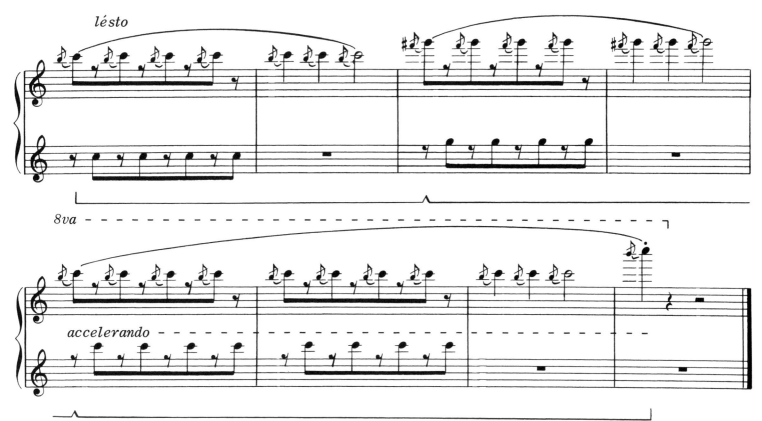

The student is ready to play this piece when he has reached page 21 of
Edna Mae Burnam's STEP BY STEP – Book Six.

LITTLE HUMMINGBIRD

By EDNA MAE BURNAM

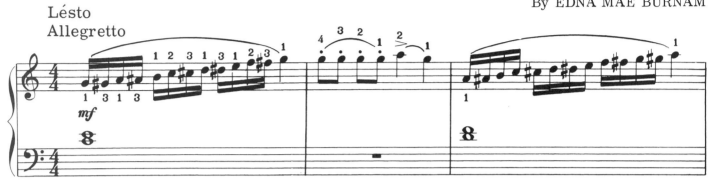

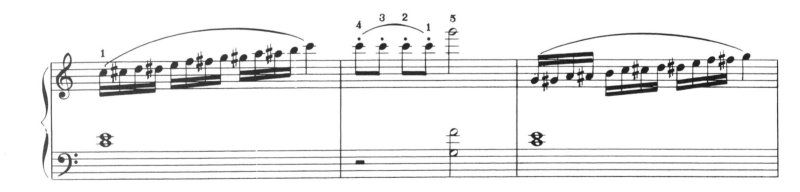

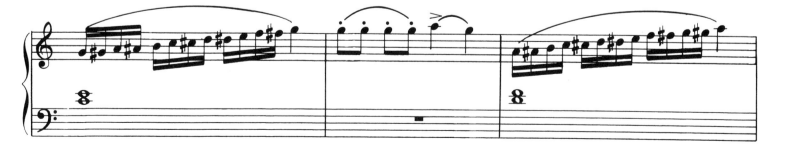

The student is ready to play this piece when he has reached page 25 of
Edna Mae Burnam's STEP BY STEP – Book Six.

GREEN PASTURES

By EDNA MAE BURNAM

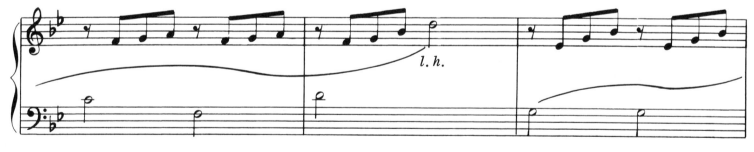

Pedal simile

The student is ready to play this piece when he has reached page 33 of
Edna Mae Burnam's STEP BY STEP – Book Six.

THE ROAD WORKERS

By EDNA MAE BURNAM

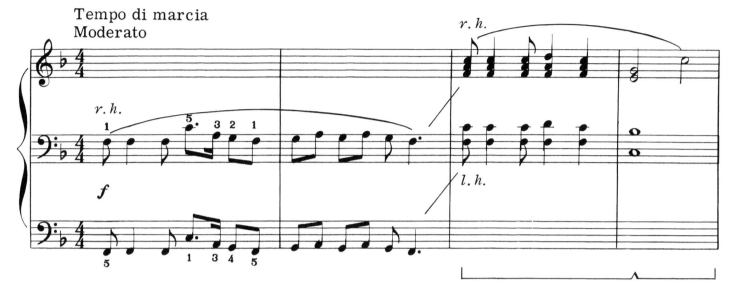

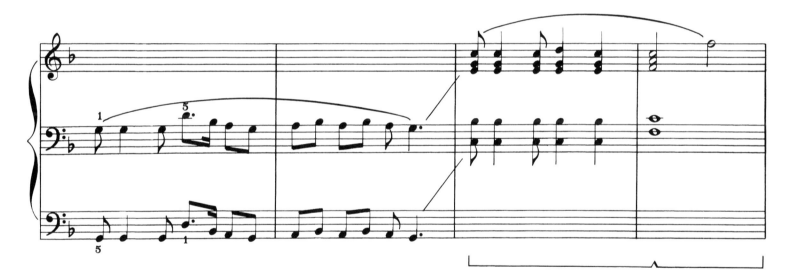

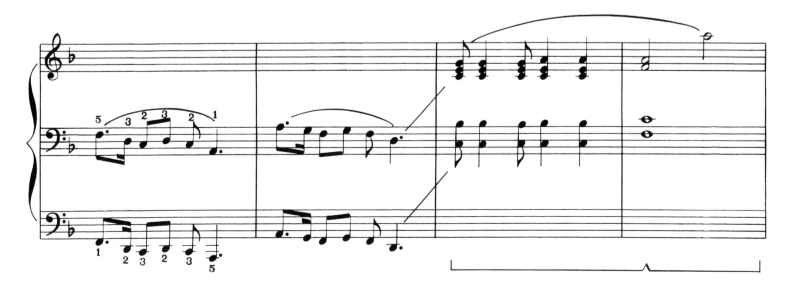

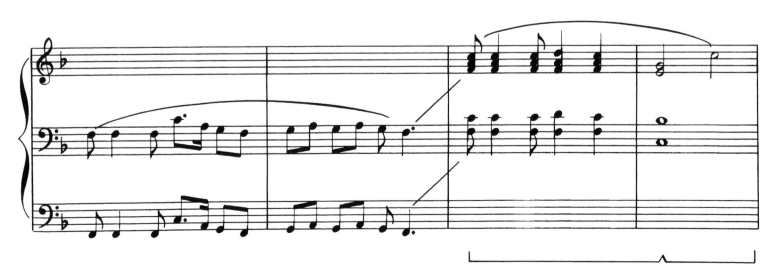

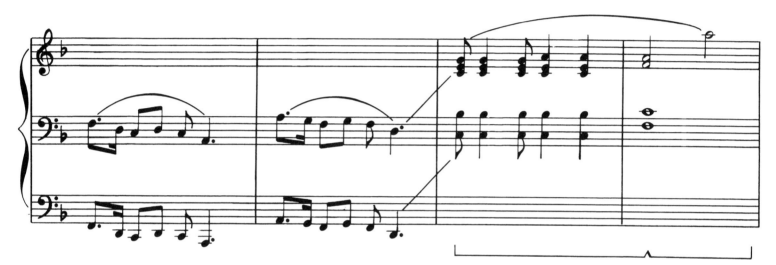

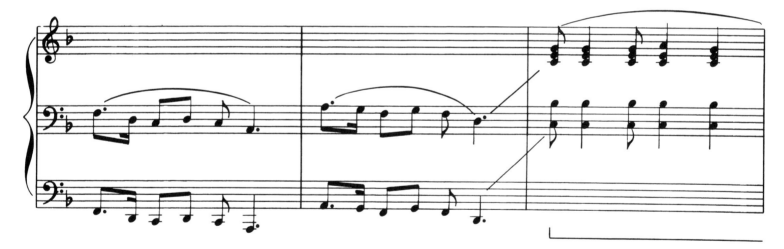

The student is ready to play this piece when he has reached page 39 of
Edna Mae Burnam's STEP BY STEP – Book Six.

FESTIVAL FUN

By EDNA MAE BURNAM

Animato
Allegro

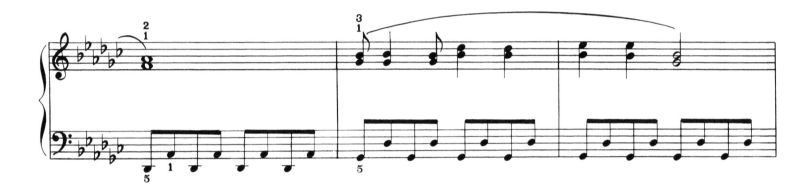

The student is ready to play this piece when he has reached page 47 of
Edna Burnam's STEP BY STEP – Book Six.

FIRESIDE THOUGHTS

By EDNA MAE BURNAM

Dolce
Andante

R.H. melody - *mf*
L.H. - *mp*

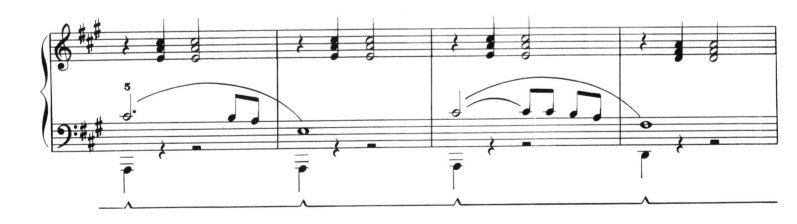

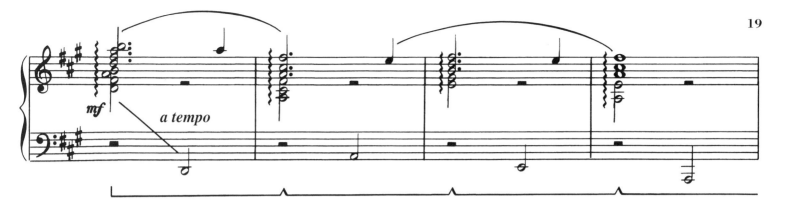

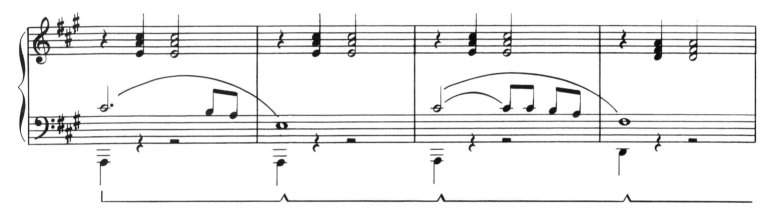

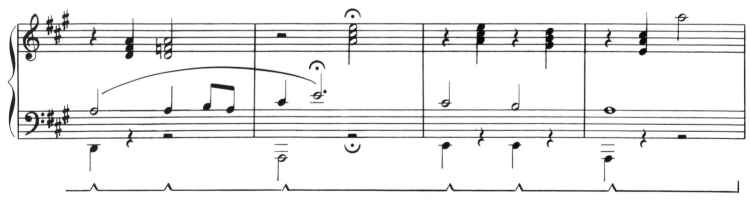

The student is ready to play this piece when he has reached page 48 of
Edna Mae Burnam's STEP BY STEP – Book Six.

SPARKLE TIME TUNE

By EDNA MAE BURNAM

15/16 Animato
Allegretto

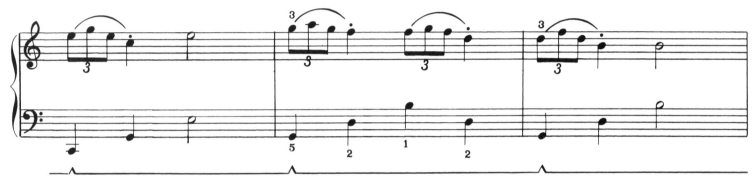

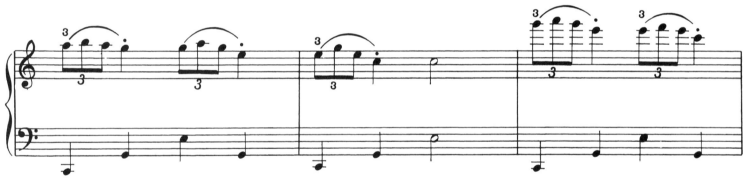

Pedal simile – to end

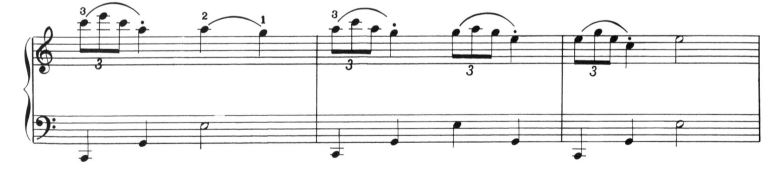

Certificate of Merit

This is to certify that

_____

has successfully completed

PIECES TO PLAY
BY
EDNA MAE BURNAM

_____Teacher

Date _____

Edna Mae Burnam

Edna Mae Burnam (1907–2007) is one of the most respected names in piano pedagogy. She began her study of the instrument at age seven with lessons from her mother, and went on to major in piano at the University of Washington and Chico State Teacher's College in Los Angeles. In 1935, she sold "The Clock That Stopped"—one of her original compositions still in print today—to a publisher for $20. In 1937, Burnam began her long and productive association with Florence, Kentucky-based Willis Music, who signed her to her first royalty contract. In 1950, she sent manuscripts to Willis for an innovative piano series comprised of short and concise warm-up exercises—she drew stick figures indicating where the "real" illustrations should be dropped in. That manuscript, along with the original stick figures, became the best-selling *A Dozen a Day* series, which has sold more than 25 million copies worldwide; the stick-figure drawings are now icons.

Burnam followed up on the success of *A Dozen a Day* with her *Step by Step Piano Course*. This method teaches students the rudiments of music in a logical order and manageable pace, for gradual and steady progress. She also composed hundreds of individual songs and pieces, many based on whimsical subjects or her international travels. These simple, yet effective learning tools for children studying piano have retained all their charm and unique qualities, and remain in print today in the Willis catalog. Visit **www.halleonard.com** to browse all available piano music by Edna Mae Burnam.